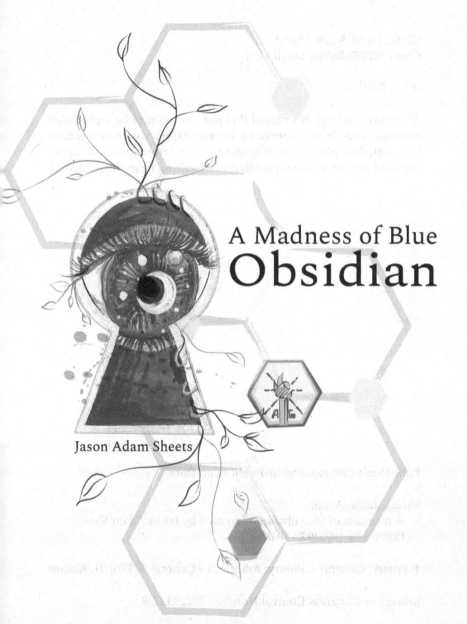

A Madness of Blue
Obsidian

Jason Adam Sheets

Publisher's Cataloguing-in-Publication Data

Sheets, Jason Adam
    A madness of blue obsidian / written by Jason Adam Sheets
    ISBN: 978-1-953932-10-5

1. Poetry: General 2. Poetry: American - General I. Title II. Author

Library of Congress Control Number: 2022932339

CONTENTS

A RING OF GHOSTS ON THE CEILING IN THE CHILD'S SILHOUETTE

CONTENTS

ALCHEMICAL FRUIT

CONTENTS

FAIRY TALES (IN THE VEIN OF THE ROSE)

CONTENTS

A RING OF GHOSTS ON THE CEILING
IN THE CHILD'S SILHOUETTE

November of Quietly Children

Notes of leafrot and husk feed an eye-birch-triple of a thing.

I've a river in hand.
You've a wreath of tombs, combs, honeycombs—

An arcanum tick of hot honey
under a birthmarked moon
here soon.

Premised by a flake of rose on pale grass, the cherry spark
of a laureate's crown defrosts.

Here, the ghost rests beneath a silent shoe. Something of an orange
flower of a swollen hour; a marble eye-
lid of discontent limed
to good cups.

You paint musical wool with a trembling paw.
I build castles of pipes on ropes of sand.

A cage of snow licks salt from scissor and skin
and the tongue: a candle, a candle in arms (the flame in the shape of a block).

A link rings alive through oblivion's red window.
I sense the hissing azaleas, barefoot on notes of leafrot and husk.

The Flowers of the Clocks Catch Fire

We've split our fruit.
We've planted sons.

You lean over a book on the kitchen table.
Your head turns a burst of white flowers
and somewhere you're wearing the turquoise dress

your mother gave to you before god shot a hole
through the wing of the bird that flew skyward
from your dream—

I found you in a church with no roof.
You drew crosses on maps that pointed to places
built to be broken.

You cup your hands.
I unbury.

Bluebell

You voice a living bone
earthworthy

and offer a finespun
apotheosis

to the animate fringe
of a tempest's dye.

What to do but still and ever forage
for your blind ghost's temple

of bluebell
in an extant grove, kissed.

Lock and Basil

There is a room
in my house of haunts

that is as thirsty
as Eden's tongue.

The door
has long since locked.

The knob's dulled.
I jam a skeleton key

into the warded lock.
My metallic desire

does not catch.
It is chewed

round by a hollow tooth
damning to click—

Through the keyhole
I see a photo of you

picking fresh basil
next to a photo of

me picking this lock
from the other side.

Kentahten (Land of Tomorrow)

My father says this gift is from my father.

A fish drops to the door
as water rushes under the house—

I leave to collect red diamonds
from colder streams afar

and will return to dig deep
to the center of them.

I could go again, to that place,
but you would not yet be here.

I remember a fog-dialed tree cave,
a toy giraffe on a broken bit of blue glass

and there, a beetle in turning
on a turning chair—

the fathering fade figured and wrapped.

JANUS

I tune to an hourglass at the bottom of the sea.

Beneath the waves, the glass sings a sufferable harmony—
that like the thinning of the human face,
that like my ghost, who sings all of his minutes away.

    [The long table knows his last great aloneness.]

He once built a ship for a woman at the foot of a mountain of scrying monkeys:

a ship in two places
twin stars of an equal birth
named—

    In a dream,
    I find the mountain and steal the name of the ship back from him.

The face of the man is never the face of the man who faces two places.
He is only deep enough when he is face down among hours,
caught in the hand like a dead clock in water.

Island of Tricks

In a morning of gossamer signature
a wry one-legged starfish points to a

string of curious relics: cowry shells
strangely aware of the sacellum below

and the painting above which explains
the condition of the sun, the condition

of the moon, the condition of unimportant
messengers in their varnish of old religion.

I pencil on a piece of brown paper bag:
The littlest worships can marble a choir

add *ruined*, perhaps, but as far as *beautiful*
is concerned, the ghosts of it raw vanquish.

Dat Rosa Mel Apibus
The Rose Gives the Bees Honey

My ghost recites a fly-in-honeyed prayer
to the shadow of a bear in a flooding cave.

If time is a key slipped under a sleeping door
I keep my key wrapped in silk under a bowl

in the kitchen:

an echo, a long truth sighing
as the sea inside pockets its waves.

Outside, a forgetful river carries a leaf
on its sky and remembers
that a tan ochre papery shrug of a thing
dissolves best in slow motion.

I find a place to overflow *sub rosa*, call on my bees
and sight a flute of forgotten weather.

In a Library of Roses

A ghost holds a rose of a forgotten color

a petal for every saint who's ever sung
from the lip of a tiger.

It twirls the stem splattering tin music,
its vespers too holy for any seeker's ear.

Knowledge is a deep well with a rickety bucket
secretly screeching *drink from within yourself*

as history begs to leave life bleeding—

to let it stain the cracks of the looking glass
as the book of each ghost it wears is bound
by a serpent ascending its own thieving spine.

It pockets the Ss and gnaws on my thorns,
gloves hands to break the planet into worth.

To Sleek a Painting

A man in a suit
floats sideways
from a white tower
toward a purpling
mountain.

A desirous lightbulb
hangs dim in a window of mouths
and wails:

tick-tock the green-sand hand hands the man

a haunted dream of the better.

so goes the shine so goes
the silver coin in the murky well—

Yes   the thickest of pulses.

The Miners

Dusk in a mining town—
a boy climbs to the top
of a lamppost on a hill
while miners stand
zigzagged in a line below:
something is and is not
right. The boy or the thing
on the lamppost fixes
or unfixes something
that is not a bulb
then something of a tailed
wandering comet kerplunks.
He wears the green aura
around his shoulders—
a moldavite hue, a varying
brightness of winking evils.
The sky rusts and becomes
dirt (save the living worm,
save the coal that the dirt
won't swallow). The miners
below toss considerations
of divine mysteries inward
then dig starward.

A Match Can Become a Witch If a Child Makes It So

She pilfers a patch of cornflowers.
She carries a storm in her mother's eye.

    She is the thing that moves through trees,
    in shock of the seed pointing downward.

She takes a bloodstone from her pocket,
skips it across a sleeping lake.

Across the lake, fireweed rings a burning trunk,
a transient grove of electric story:

    The fire fell from the claw of the bird with many masks.
    On a ritual mask, the mouth can be omitted.

A fish belongs to the lake.
A fish her father was never able to eat.

The fish's gaze hangs in the air like a paper banner—

    Did you know you can harness the energy of a cloud
    if you pluck the eyes from the fingers of the nun
    whose face is a window?

Breton saw a man cut in two by the window.
The man was a fish seeking thunder in piles of sticks.

    She learned to count the sticks ...

and pomegranates: fruit's frequent potential:
the space within seeds is measured by need.

She sails through the strings of a harp, her apparition.

She jumps into an eclipse off a cliff that becomes an arm—
See, she's died twice with seeds in her teeth-teeth-teeth.

For Rubén Darío

I've seen the divine cantharus
adrift white in the tide's navel
buoyant and brazenly moved
by its own movement—

Even after you died, you heard its words
and remained

a true rhapsodomancy in the shape
of a heart.

Your melancholy was cut from Argo's white sail
first pierced by the dart of a nocturne still sung
by your celestial bull.

The azure cord around the alb's waist remains
tied to the star that blessed my brain's reveries.

Something Tender Then Will Leap

Should the sun
set sideways
in the midst
of our scattered parts:

let us hook a fish
from a clear river
of stars

and water clockwise
this thought-flower sufficient
as becomings belong
to the shape of living things.

Let us tend to the song
of the sunken stones.
Let us quietly color
olive or cherry

that which we
long to outlive—

something tender
then will leap:
a secret rabbit
in silvery Time

eyeing.

We have
only this much
in common:

we come
then become
keepers of things.

You set fire
to a wreck of dire roses
and flicker
like an ever-burning lamp

fueled by the charm
of a deeper system.

I pluck wild pearls
from the quick ends
of branches

as desire becomes
that which turns widely
to diminish—

that which becomes
an altar becomes
altered becomes

a quiet turning
between two mirrors.

Let us wonder
if the painter of whorls
will spill a rivered thing
once more

from where
we have hidden ourselves
in the making

before the parts
that have already been—

Violin (Red Asters)

a tone crescent
from the throat
of the violin
is the photo
of you
glossing
your lip

the note
costumes
red asters
halts
in midair
becomes frozen
in the bloom of you

Brocken Spectre

On the edge of a haze
the open world closes
before them as if they
were the thing hidden

in the disc of a shell
or the cap of a kernel.

Before they know
what they would come
to know they hold torches

to the painted roof of a cave
and see that which
is only seeking
its own existence.

Their question mark
hangs behind a hooked Ą—

All potent things desire
to be close to existing.

Earthen

(plucks skull from the dirt)

all and we
were sculptures

origin figures
with the ability

to remove our
faces at the nose

wherein fresh soil
and budding bulbs

would spill living
onto the fresh floor of the world

Thief in the Reeds

thunder thumps
the ashy river alive

and the tempest of the cold
beige breaks into me

a field of poppies
lavender or sapphire

and eyes of an apple's heart—
a horse licks the living core

and scattering off he scatters
me soft to the thief in the reeds

ALCHEMICAL FRUIT

The Art Of

the art of	the pearl never found
the art of	the glazed ghost in rain
the art of	the seer of the open bone
the art of	the embryonic note to Self
the art of	the vibrating instrument
the art of	the doctrine still veiled
the art of	the vital liquid pure enough to drink
the art of	the seed as it appears and reappears
the art of	the realm of the sun's influence
the art of	the Rose Croix and the jade bezel
the art of	the four-handed astronomical clock
the art of	the glass cube hovering above the ocean
the art of	the vanishing rind on a buddha of dunes
the art of	the eye looking back	kcab gnikool eye eht

Vastu Nine

A blue thread drifts
across black and white tile

as a priest (named after a fish)
feeds grasshoppers
frozen in ice

to three dangling animals
gone blind: they suspend

language—

I kneel in the realm
of wild supplicants.

Seven

in a pure dent of its shade

        a tinny hook mirrors in slow spin

weaving a thunderstone lock of the mouth

        needle needling needless need needy needles needlelike

the little keyed whorls seven a crispness

        seven the (curious) knots of brittle crosses

pinned savage to their blazing yellow selves

Hermetic Math

turtle is the number 15
between moons
blue is 4 and there are 3
heavenly substances
of harmonic proportions
sulphur mercury salt
the azoth of the sages
which determine
the number of wheels
in your bag
a lady and her unicorn
are 12 and there are 13
birds in each day
which sing to the 9
lords of night
from the 8th orb and counting

Atop a Cliff of Heliotropic Lamps

17 sunflowers an olfaction
a heaven in the middle
of Babel a sea
of seeds 72 seeds
where all 54 eyelids
blink a flame to sleep
to see a seed flaming
to seed a sight christened
the trumpet blue sound
of honorary red syrups
as they coat the throat
of a body while its fist
holds a shield
never a more ossified pigment
how the color of thunder tints
the cleary clanking lamps of the pine

The Oracular Lark

pinks the way
of the eyeless

toward a slat
zodiac of beaks
ever trilling

in foxfire
in spaces to wither

evanescing
it finds its worm
in a shrine of little chirps

At Aphelion

an entity
in clay is
a sea-clay
cloning
a wheeled
thing eaten
is a root
in a bottle
a fruition
uncanny
is a laugh-
able arc
as be-
comings
belong
name
them
a thing
ecliptic

Eye

rise from the eye
of the bending
wing

an ivory vulture
moves within you

consumes with you

Palm

Twice bitten
by the bird of many colors

first felt and named
from beneath its wing—

from its eye
comes an instantaneous cube
an unalterable thing.

The sky conjures living things.

Within a star-drunk wind
low to the shrunken
made to be shrunken

you remove your hand from the palm.

You are not burdened
but still you burn
for more and fire holy

a prayer a heat godly
toward the waiting mouth.

The Shadow and the Dove

An egg falls out of her pocket.

She lights a raspberry lamp
and embodies geometry embodying itself.

Her shadow contains the essence
and a dove.

The dove cooing how a changeling coos
soothes her.

Axis of Pinkness

ice-prints
plum stones
lone rosettes
and riverlight

hinged to the axis of pinkness

quartzed
flamingoed
clockwise
without form

bubbles a sequence

a spooning medallion
of animated water
the instrumental hush
of the opener of seeds

Estuary

on the neck of the wolf
a burning stacked

a plant of ash
spreads a night-shining
cloud

a call to the humors
a lucent feud

a cordial sorcery
as two crabs
fight for their mate

Consider the Shades

I pluck a comet of memory
from the thick lake of being

and some black-milked mottled
decantation of you skims me.

I tell it to the glare
of a spinning claw

from where there are
two kinds of blood
two kinds of ribs

from where fire
and rosewater
meet the mirage
or device
of this moon's
naked eye—

I clothe the coaled wind blank.

Featherful

a featherful night
fathers the shine
of the crow of
a deeper voice
in limbo and
in harmony
with the children
of soil and song
a velveteen tune
of being and been
of having been
numbered 4
of having been buried
safe under a dust

Oranging

Of what
belongs
most
to the
orange
promise
of air

of what
we wear
for one
another
kindly
or
frayed.

A
fold.
A
hand.
A
mockery

of a
dead
carnival
of
night's
shine:

a weaving,
familiar.

Zodiacal Light

There are four perfects
strung waterish.

The two fish of Pisces
lay at the feet
of the grand solar man.

His fish lie hid:
they swim
through the earth
are dug from the earth
and placed in the minds of things.

To a Poet (Akashic)

"In a hundred years,
we shall see your name
on our story."

Drink your milk from one stone
and be merry like poppies in rain
for time will unbury your memory
dressed at once in its finest blue.

Look to the shore for the waters
your two hearts thirst
and find your stone—
it will not turn its back on you.

Hold your world at eye level
and see how all things are cast
by the snake in the rainbow
dreaming.

Pray for the thousandth dart
—as you shuffle through the color
of the world—and all the stars
will rise to blink you a melody.

Numina

float
upon
themselves

serve
symbols
of fire

on
saucers

of
bone

to
the
shined

when
will

the
horse's
water
sleep?

FAIRY TALES (IN THE VEIN OF THE ROSE)

Stoneward

An origin spirit tucked in a tree-
hollow flits with an elemental
hunger for the fruit of a seed.
Red unthreads from its wrist
as an auric garden reveals
its landscape: igneous stone
stairs cooled to a smooth slide.
In the distance, three shined
wooden boats pose vertical
on a paradisiacal sea as a bale
of young turtles tend wildly
to their visions. The red thread
on the cooled lava becomes a
freshet hurrying toward the sea
where there is no word for how
an ivory whelk lying on sand looks
when eyed through clear water.

Red Sprites

On the airy lid of the world
splinters of crystal suspend
an electric myth:

The first daughters came here
in the form of red lightning—

their voices shook sea from sky.

Their mother the mother of color
whose wings unfeathered the dye
made all of them red in her image
from a table in a daughterless sky.

The Windmill

On a balcony
near the edge
of the woods
an anchoress
unweaves
her altarpiece:

elk, fauna,
fragments,
sap and white berries.

She is of a mossy origin.

To reverse
her magnificent
purgatory

she takes two dolls
nailed to a wooden boat
to the windmill
in the woods and weeps.

The Painter

Into the slits
a painter
carries a box of books
down a darkened hall.

One tells of a
familiar
pandemonium

(anamnesis)

another,
a memoried tome
(*mi ritrovai*).

He carries his brushes
in a thick bag
by his side

leaves the books
with the poets
and paints a color
no good god could mind.

The Carver

The eye of the circumpunct

        stares back
        plinian and sunned.

The old story (of its sleep) is written now.

The carver, starry in the story:

        After enlightenment,
        one knows the blue flame that bitters the palm—
        the burden of both, of having survived none.

Centipede (Five Suns)

A black and white centipede climbs into a jar and eats the five suns of poetry.
In its belly, the suns become waves that push all the good rocks back to shore.

Beneath the rocks are the futures of their work.

The King's Jar

There is a fragment of a poem in a small clay jar buried in sand.
A young king finds it and declares it a poem worth
burning:

Heed the heavenly horn of harmony,

The bellring of thy hearer's holy hand,

For the sand offers nothing but ruin,

In the vein of the rose goes the King's plan.

A blistering portent, an auspice aflame. The thing in the jar
needs burning. Yes, it needs burning, this the king
is aware.

The Fisherman (Omen)

A string of stone beads
is plucked from the sea
by the fisherman home
in his mirrored abyss.

A cradle of turnings
in an energetic wake pools
then sinks—

To catch the true nature
of one's omen:

Position a libation. Pour.

Prize the catch
(like a vessel of fish)
plucked backward
from the wink of the arch.

Unmoored, tell cold.

Heartwood & Bone: Three Siblings

I

He plunges his hands into the river and guddles a slippery fish. He cradles it awhile eyeing the curious color of the thing. He lets it swim into his right eye. He thanks the fish for giving him the curious color, then paints a blind rivery eye.

II

Tucked behind a grassy knoll alongside his brother, he throws icy spears of light at wicked green flying things plummeting down toward them. That evening, after bread and black wine, he makes legs of stained glass and sings to them.

III

The sister is a seamstress who lives in a starlit dome. She spends her idyllic days spooling each of brother's little deaths from afar. Each night, after she has collected all of their little deaths, she levitates diamondlike blue then twitches goodbye.

The Grinning Snake

A snake grins from eye to eye.
A girl strolling by
spots the snake and looks it in the eye.

The snake does not scare her.

She grins at the grinning snake
no longer afraid of the wicked
and in sun becomes a book of glass.

The Shepherd's Bell

a seedpod of a sacral
flower from the sun's
navel is to be drunk
with honey or wine

      a bird in a waterspout
      is a tongue sewn to the sky

in every seed is a sun
etched on a weathered bell
housed in a shepherd's kitchen

    ...

the shepherd collects
stones from a rainful circle
climbs to a summit
and hangs his bell
signaling to the elements
to strike and flourish threefold

a packed causation

      fetch a pool of sheep
      gather strength in air
      and carry it to others
      as a flowing forth flows

    ...

the shepherd falls into white
his bell rings
in the ear of a euphonious god

Hermes
plucks silvery threads of a lyre
and law thaws

snow pierces the shepherd's sky
inward

he knows the figbird's offing heart
he knows the omen

     it is a good thing
     it is
     what a thawing thing
     looks like

when an ivory prayer
melts on the tongue
like a verse drowning in good water

...

Iris folds her hands

Hermes' one thing
is accomplished and ended

a dweller of the innermost
a clanking nary slice

     the shepherd
     of the dreamtime

his twinned rainbow
a gleaming handle in place

Elephant & Fig

Elephant is born with a white ring around her left eye at the zenith
of a solar eclipse.

Fig peels some bark from a firetree.
He crushes berries
& madder root into an ink
& scribes
the auspicious event.

As the ink dries, the white ring around Elephant's
eye becomes the next ring within the firetree
& she is reborn
Lady of the Tree.

The Makers

The makers   ABRACADABRA
climb everlasting stalks   ABRACADABR
a glittery blue crop   ABRACADAB
of musical masts   ABRACADA
                               ABRACAD
stone-folk of an æther   ABRACA
alone and fully real   ABRAC
                               ABRA
their book written   ABR
in an aeon of twining   AB
is a spontaneous birth   A
of radiant keeping.

They build their boat
from star to star
anchor to the antler
of Orion: an illustrious art

an abracadabra
and the core
the glassy core—

In an open eye
(fluent to matters)
one reads:

To unmake the world, find the center of a thought.

They are the authors
of a double unpeopling

the builders of shipwrecks
of tin-packed stars.

Virga

A hummingbird
flies backward
through a cave
of painted bulls
appearing only
when paused
in wet light.

A crown spider
crawls out of a hole
commanding rain—

vapor is a time
when all sound
becomes human

when the white eye of life

writes law on a feather
writes sin on an arrow

to middle the names carved
in the hidden.

THE M POEMS

Magnetic Room

By what rains do I—

    the [telling] clock in the tide
    the [telling] structure of ash
    the [telling] horn beneath windowglass

A wave swells toward me

                                          or no

but I am in a room and from the sideways slant of this yellow corner can
the wilted leaf cherrying, the spoon in the bowl, how the three seem to ha
themselves from my vision or have themselves I do not know if one made thi
can own another and I wonder if I could complete another living thing I me
compete with no I mean complete—I look out of the window's windowglass a wa
swells toward me carrying with it a story that beg-ends with a circular thud tw
dissolved in the eye of some living thing and O by what rains do I *I* and why did
I know you   when I was ali

Mad Statue Sudden

Not the mouse but the shadow of the mouse
quickens beneath whiskey, cello, white thorn—

The mark of a living thing, asking.

If I hold an imaginary shell to a real ear
and peek at strawberries in cracked glass
and ask them if they know
who drank my drought

and if you hold a real shell to an imaginary ear
and gaze at the splay of a stilling wine
while lamenting about some great obscurity

will a row of black houses on a lid of yellow grass
work to accomplish an operatic distance
and the miracle of once-living things on return?

On a wall behind you, there is a chattering eye,
a final body, a grave of zeros, a portrait
of a sphinx that makes room.

Behind me, a pot full of matches lit at wrong ends.

Tonight, you brush your hair in the bend of a mother's
mirror while I unpocket coins from a place
I've never been, traveling until then to what
blinks at the source.

Magnoliastory

The red lion traces its paw
below the branches of forgiving
gold

while newborn beams of silver
light dispense their hours

as rowan berries on the plate
of the day.

Sleepers
once awoke to a peal of bells
in a thin city here

their planetary hours
sweet as honey cakes.

Their divinity
now stretched twice
toward the sun—
two ghosts on stilts.

There is still kindling
of horsehair and white plumage
a doorkeeper
in the shape of a yellow horse

a yearling's galloping wish
at the base.

Milkstone

You breathe through a body of many bodies.

Reborn the hunted or the trickster
you hold a milkstone to a clear flame
and pray good-drunk on the magic water of music.

Your aged rose in cricketsong meets one of two
gardens, the song of yourself sowing along:

If we don't sing the words, we'll stop hearing them.

Inhale the images
but do not speak them from a homesick throat.

For what it's worth, we have both become
that which again we will leave behind

so tell me a sparkle lucky, in the opaque metronome
of moondusted fog reaching for your reaching hand—

Milliner

The five petals of Venus
fall to the threshing floor
as night-birds in an alcove
flick with their beaks
circlets of straw starward—

A widow in a crimson cloak,
her face hid behind a black veil,
pulls strands of wet silver
from her creaking loom—

[Her power is]
to open what is shut;
to shut what is open.

She glints at her red-capped
little hours—
noble and sororal—
as the nightjars sing
for her the secret life
of the maker in the made.

Mella

I see that the girl in the garden is not the girl
in the roses, not my wistful muse who drinks
her honey from a pink cup—this one drinks
a rootstock concoction with a frenetic thirst
I discern only a clock could quell. Tucked
behind a golden-faced grove of orange trees,
she extracts their stars—the number
of which exceeds belief—my flowers begin
to grow downward in hues of latent change.
The girl's handgrown Book is a vine on my
window striving to ascend beyond the stale
need of things here: she walks on a ground
of many worlds, earth caked to her toes,
germinating the seeds of who I will be with
each step. No, there is not a girl in the roses,
only the girl in the garden, who declares that
I and the rest of who I am will gradually die
into her perennial astronomy of future events.

Memory Red

sew a tone
to your view
then watch
as summer
hail turns
to apples
turning
to tiny red
memories
fruiting
their way
toward
your
earth
yes in
all things
splayed
by blank
gravities
or pursed
irreal in
the clasp
of a city's
light you
will find
the muse-
sick music
the red-
jeweled
shine from
which you
must work

Metanoia

Silvergrass and deep sky objects
ejected from the hush of a dream

playfully thieved by a maddening
sheen organic.

I awake to a pure beach of eyes,
opaleyes, water-gnomes, one as Desdemona

who recalls for me sullenly the rudiments
of Nature's final belief:

coral a combination of locked cosmos
or better, the urchin, the panacea

for the necrotic bits that descend, or float by—

a theatre of crabs in an arctic attic
is a counterfeit colony of blind buttons

sewn to the skeletons of their lovers—how we
shed, en route, the soul of our native stations.

At the end of this universe I am alive at sea level,
ebbed fast awake in an audience of symbols.

Mothlike

what is missing is that which can be missed
what is missing is that which can be missed
what is missing is that which can
what is missing is that
what is missing is
what is—

I pillage the bones and make homes of what could be.

I see you riding or the ghost of you riding an animal of your
choosing an animal I have not seen before in this world and there
are two fires of varying intensity one in the lower dwelling of a
psychic landscape you know better than I and the other in what
moves freely and there is a third I dare not write but imagine a lawn
of quickening ash or a labyrinth of ash evoking its own embers in
air and in the structure of ash there is a telling where two make
home to one and yes how shiny it would be to bring Dickinson's
bees into this scene but that cannot happen here it would be the
same as my telling you about the twin bells you'd sent to me after
you died but it's not in light to share those so I will continue to use
this flickering stage to write my way into you this way it's true and
somewhere I would already have destroyed this or poured enough
water on it to diminish its flame but what is the fun in drowning a
thing when I cannot taste the thing the dream drinks or the image
that has funnelled its way into the sleeping eye of this page so I
now ask it to send me to places where bone turns to home.

Gertrude Stein would make broth from the bone and I imagine
that Duncan and Hughes would have a good spoon and I wonder
what they would say to this contemporariness and I wonder if they
would bring their blocks and bags and occulting orbs of vision or if

they would stay behind and far away from this crude and scratched language now since they know too well that English is an ugly language how it writes itself away from the ancient way of things away from left to right away from the page and onto the screen if I were to have written this by hand on good paper I imagine I would have a small thing to say and perhaps more purposed as my hand isn't as careful here when it's not attached to thin lead but this is how the old stories are now written and perhaps I delight in the thirst it quenches and the tinny web it weaves through the dark fire of a mind and this isn't to say that all fires are bad or destructive hell these surely aren't they are good as a god and in dreams the image of fire is considered a blessing and I only dream of fire after someone close to me has died.

My window is cracked and there is a snowstorm outside burying bones I could not carry and the cold wind is good yes good as a god and I know that it's real because my candle is flickering.

PENETRALIA | FRAGMENTS

The high trace of you

                in the trace of the clock

ruptures the difference.

A photograph of a feather in the mail

                              bent

says that I can only feel one pain by doing that—

                              my ability to engine

                                    is premised.

the impish almanac whistles a hiss
a kettle of tea a kiss of boiling keys

spread the heat in all its asking

Thirteenth wheel a Zone—   butterfly eggs.

The red door facing west is covered in ants.

The stone melts the human word,

A
geode
sunbow
thorntree
birdboned
bonesmoked
bloodwatered
toadstool
salt

uncooled at highest intensity.

arils   panpipes

lamb   an action
                         of razors

toiling coil of oil   plunk

river of gold dust   drip drop

Pan panning

water on the lace is the water in the jar
water on the lace is the water in the jar
water on the lace is the water in the jar

a slight tilt of the sharp   a slight tilt of the sharp
a slight tilt of the sharp   write your way into
                                 your way in two

I found you when no one was speaking
I found you when no one was speaking

how tight taught the rope

how tight taught the rope

how tight taught the rope

more than a question the apostrophized word of

do what you must and leave what you will
do what you must and leave what you will

The smoke of your blank in an envelope
but not what you think.

My celestial bull is a white buffalo riding waves in a grain of sand.
                              [eclipse]

twice tick the triangle third
twice tick the triangle third
twice tick the triangle third

knack   the tick
splice thick the angle
of birth   under-eyed

the shine fits the shine fits the shine fits

H spicket horseshoe

and so it begins
and so it begins
and so it begins
so the ground on the inside splits

the flower house →

tap the tongue in all its wagging
tap the tongue in all its wagging
                              show the boat

a tomato red in inkling pollen
inking pollen   flit

what does the color bring to this place
what does the color bring to this place

a madness of blue obsidian
a madness of blue obsidian

You never know what one recalls twice on Mars.

One arm through the gate
a thing watery wanes and halves bright on the occulting orb of vision—

A black bee gathers pollen from a flower of ash.

"Make bread from a flour of ash."

In flour one finds *ash*, the mineral content that remains after burning the whole.

Purification by fire reveals hidden essences: the worker
robed against
the longest bridge

irenic fritillaries and a porcupine's
                              quill drift

the wind winds the wilding sand
the wilding sand winding a road
the sand knows the wind's wilds

tincture project-

ion a pinch of coal on the eyelid blank
a pinch of coal on the eyelid blank

they see me   blue

sugar clump a far clay hay sugar bury a stack sweetpea
a needle so that

sliver the mime in time he'll talk
sliver the mime in time he'll talk

walk backward with a gallon of milk

taste the hair of the hare
peculiar
tease it there

it has no use for you

[What are the rules for your uses?]

So what if the world. The gray stain in rain plump from the look of it.

flip burn flip burn flip burn
now fish

a scale for the walking   talks the most
the horror   the horror

ham in a shoe   trust not

a pencil pulse of drastic measure
a maddening   pigeon suffused

Triple the lock three at the static.
Triple the lock three at the static.

Radio door nervous.

Half in the way of you.

I.

Half in the way of you.

[Something supposes that it is done.]

glass spine   boat less broken

an orange lament on the skin of a heel
an orange lament on the skin of a heel
a good meal on green sober   a dance

slink the limes
in heavenly water
choke the mote splendid

a wisp of a ghost
a wisp of a ghost

a bit of orange thread
brights the page

The distance of grief becomes purple. A purple in crimson dripped slow. A blue teacup adds a bit. Orange pulp. Subtract the brown not earthy. Spit.

A lip of a man who kills his mice.

                              a volcano becomes a turtle
                         joy becomes gasoline I have seen
                    the islands in dream—a mirror yours

A crab has my pen ...

pickling in a pool of language ...

a box with an X in it
asks what the sharp thing wants
I cannot offer it E
(blue belongs to E)
and I cannot offer it yellow
(which is 7)
so X can stay in its box
and does what it does best

a month of perfume
a moth's legume

clutch   a notice, lowtide

seep there

bundle the twigs a cross will do
bundle the twigs a cross will do
poke in dirt   a croft, kind

Two blue flames of a name
Two blue flames of a name
A chest of burns turns north
        the owlet nightjar
        the owlet nightjar
        runs rain to the nearest drop

last street was too vivid for me tomorrow

waterlogged cross hidden lever
stump of stones lichened levels

Tape the eyes of one last ghost.

Who knows what they've seen him do.

NOTES

"The Flowers of the Clocks Catch Fire"

> This title is borrowed from Tristan Tzara's poem, "The Great Lament of My Obscurity Three."

"A Match Can Become a Witch If a Child Makes It So"

> This title is a paraphrase of a section of a paper on "the force of the daemonic world of childhood," written by ethnologist and archaeologist Leo Frobenius.

"Eye"

> The line, "rise from the eye of the bending wing," is borrowed from *The Dawning Moon of the Mind* by Susan Brind Morrow.

"To a Poet (Akashic)"

> The line, "pray for the thousandth dart," is a nod to Rubén Darío's poem, "Melancholy."

> The line, "shuffle through the color of the world," is borrowed from Tristan Tzara's poem, "The Great Lament of My Obscurity Three."

"Centipede (Five Suns)"

Inspired by Sri Aurobindo's "five suns of poetry": Truth, Beauty, Delight, Life, and Spirit.

"The Makers"

The line, "To unmake the world, find the center of a thought," is borrowed from *The Dawning Moon of the Mind* by Susan Brind Morrow.

ACKNOWLEDGEMENTS

Thank you to the editors of *Figroot Press*, *The Harpoon Review*, *Apricity Press*, *Mantra Review*, *The Graduate Journal of Harvard Divinity School*, and *Fare Forward*, for being the first to believe in these poems.

My gratitude to The Oxford Research Centre in the Humanities, for featuring "Something Tender Then Will Leap" and "Lock and Basil" in their digital reading series.

Whether through space or time, my deep abiding gratitude to the many poets and seers whose visions and words helped to inspire and sustain the making of this book—thank you.

ABOUT THE POET

Jason Adam Sheets is the author of *The Hour Wasp* (2017) and co-author of *Theopoetica: A Micro-Anthology* (2022). He is the recipient of the 2016 Poetry Society of New Hampshire Poetry Prize. His poems have appeared in numerous journals and magazines and have most recently been featured by The Oxford Research Centre in the Humanities and *The Graduate Journal of Harvard Divinity School*. He has taught in Harvard's Poetry in America for High Schools Program and has worked as a mentor for AWP's writer to writer mentorship program. His work has been supported by Harvard University, PEN America, and Poets & Writers.